T·J·PUBLIS

ILLUSTRATIONS BY / FRANK ALLEN P
RESEARCH ILLUSTRATOR / THE SALK INSTIT
LA JOLLA / CALIFOR

SIGNS
OF SEXUAL
BEHAVIOR

AN INTRODUCTION TO SOME SEX-RELATED
VOCABULARY IN AMERICAN SIGN LANGUAGE

BY JAMES WOODWARD

Cover and book design by FRANK ALLEN PAUL

© 1979, JAMES WOODWARD

T.J. PUBLISHERS, INC.
817 Silver Spring Avenue, 206 / Silver Spring,
Maryland 20910

Printed in the United States of America

ISBN 0-932666-02-7
Library of Congress Catalog No.: 79-84495

First printing April 1979
Second printing June 1979
Third printing March 1982
Fourth printing August 1986

DEDICATION

I dedicate this book to members of the U.S. Deaf community in the sincere hope that it will ultimately prove beneficial.

All royalties from this book will be used to establish and maintain a non-profit sign language research institute. This institute, Sign Language Research, Inc., is new and independent from any existing institutions or organizations. Research focus will be on sign languages as they are used in Deaf communities throughout the world.

CONTENTS

ACKNOWLEDGEMENTS

It is impossible to give appropriate credit to all individuals responsible for this publication because of the large number of people involved in this project and especially because of the need to protect the rights of consultants. However, I want to single out some individuals for special thanks. I would first like to thank all of the Deaf consultants who worked with me, the two Deaf models, and the Deaf people who helped me locate the models. Second, thanks go to David Smith, who shared with me his sensitivities for and appreciation of cultural differences and supplied me with a framework for discussing the importance of such differences.

Next, I would like to thank T.J. O'Rourke who was instrumental in getting me involved in the initial collection, periodic presentation, and final publication of these signs of sexual behavior. In addition, I wish to express appreciation to Carol Erting and Susan De Santis who helped me at various times in data collection and especially to Susan De Santis who provided encouragement. Finally, I want to thank Lloyd Anderson, Charlotte Baker, Susan De Santis, Kitty Dillman, Robert Dillman, David Peterson and William Stokoe for their comments and criticisms on the written text of this book.

Any insensitivities or inaccuracies are my responsibility alone.

Research on White and Black Southern signs was supported in part by NSF Research Grant SOC74-14724.

INTRODUCTION

The semantic area dealt with in this book is of a very sensitive nature. I debated with myself for a long time before I agreed that the advantages of publishing the book outweighed the disadvantages. These signs are used by core members of the Deaf community in intimate interaction with other core members of the Deaf community. As I discuss later, these signs seem to serve an important function in maintaining ethnic identity in the Deaf community. By exposing these signs to the public, I, a Hearing researcher, am in fact revealing an intimate part of the Deaf community to Hearing outsiders, who may not be sensitive to the needs and desires of Deaf people. A number of Deaf people I have talked with have indicated ambivalent feelings about sharing such signs with Hearing people, since the Deaf people felt that these signs belong to intimate interaction among members of the Deaf community. More important, perhaps, is that some of these Deaf people also indicated that a number of Hearing people they have known tried to learn and use signs related to sexual behavior. These Hearing people were not interested in learning other signs. Moreover, the Hearing people constantly used these signs in a derogatory and mocking fashion. Such a derogatory use of signs seems to be an indicator of Hearing people's negative attitudes towards and negative stereotypes of Deaf people (Woodward 1975). I in no way wish to be a partner to such oppressive activities, yet by making information on these signs readily available, I may in fact be exposing Deaf people to the possibility of more oppression (see Vernon 1972).

There are advantages, however, to dissemination of this material. Interpreters, who in general are not very knowledgeable about such signs (Woodward 1977), will be better able to serve Deaf people. One anecdotal example related to me by a Deaf man should suffice to illustrate the situation. A Deaf defendant in a trial for rape was asked, "Did you want to rape this woman?" The interpreter, not knowing a sign for rape, translated, "Did you want to have intercourse with this woman?" These questions are worlds apart.

In addition, non-English materials for sex education are sorely lacking for Deaf individuals. A number of Hearing parents especially need and want information for sex education (Max Fitzgerald, Sex Education Specialist, Kendall School).

The fact that Deaf people have been and could be involved in trials related to serious crimes while many interpreters do not have appropriate knowledge of sexual signs, the fact that good sex education materials for Deaf children are lacking, and the fact that signed information on birth control, venereal disease, etc. are not readily available for Deaf people convinced me that the possible advantages of this book outweigh the possible disadvantages. I can only urge prospective users of this book to handle the important information in this book with extreme sensitivity to the needs of the Deaf community.

LANGUAGE ATTITUDES AND SEXUAL SIGNS

Sociolinguistic attitudes must be positive, if adequate communication and interpreting services are to result. There should be respect for all languages in the communication situation. Cross cultural judgements must be avoided. The sign INTERCOURSE, made with two "V" handshapes, is often translated into English as 'fuck'. However, the sign does not have the same force in American Sign Language (ASL) as the English word. Some Deaf people may fingerspell F-U-C-K, if they do not know the English word 'intercourse'. To many Deaf people, who are not usually native in English, and for whom English is a learned language, like Latin is to Hearing people, English 'fuck' does not have the same connotations as it does for Hearing people, whose language is English. Similarly, Hearing people may use one sign for oral sex only to learn that Deaf people find that sign very impolite. If the Hearing people had been native or known other variants, the communication problem would have been avoided. The whole point is that Hearing people cannot judge an ASL translation of an English word the same way that they judge the English word. The sign and word belong to two different languages and value systems. (If in doubt, remember that the worst thing a Chinese person can call another is a 'stupid egg' or 'turtle egg'. It is on par with English 'bastard' but much worse.)

Often Hearing people ethnocentrically consider English better than ASL and will try to invent new signs if they do not know an ASL sign for an intended meaning. However, it is much easier and more logical to ask Deaf people what the sign is. If some Deaf people do not have a sign that meets the English definition, Deaf people from other regions of the country will probably have a sign. It is always preferable from a linguistic point of view to use existing words within a language than to try to invent new words for language standardization. For example, if a Deaf person does not understand fingerspelled R-A-P-E, he/she will not understand an invented artificial sign that is used by no Deaf person. Interpreters should always be aware of what people in their own community are using. Perhaps two examples of Hearing people inventing signs will illustrate my point. I know of one preschool teacher who invented a very nice sign for fountain. It happened to be identical to one of the signs for EJACULATION. Deaf children of Deaf parents might go home and they might talk about the nice fountain at school. Parents might be a little concerned about what is happening in that classroom. Also, I know of some people who tried to invent a sign for 'beanstalk' as in 'Jack and the Beanstalk'. Instead of asking Deaf people, they developed what they felt to be a very nice 'iconic' sign, but it did not happen to be appropriate since this is one of the less polite signs for ERECTION-OF-PENIS. So Jack and his Beanstalk might carry some unintended connotations.

In a rape case, similar mistakes to the ones mentioned above could prove disastrous. Very real problems can arise from not finding out what signs Deaf individuals in a given community use. There is a great deal of variation in signs.

SOME CAUTIONS WITH DATA COLLECTION

The only way to communicate effectively with Deaf people is to find out what language forms they use in a given community. The only way to find out is to actually talk with a number of Deaf individuals with various educational backgrounds and social roles in the community. This can be fairly easy, however, there are some pitfalls that should be avoided.

Some Deaf people are reluctant to show these signs to Hearing people. The following situations will increase Deaf people's reluctance: The Hearing person does not explain the purpose for which the signs will be used; the Hearing person has strong connections with an organized church, especially one that Deaf people are involved in; the Hearing person is totally incompetent in sexual signs; and/or the Hearing person is a very poor signer.

One way to approach the situation is to explain that the signs will be used for interpreting purposes, especially in court cases such as rape. To loosen things up a bit, the Hearing person should carefully try to demonstrate some of the sexual signs he/she had seen, asking Deaf people if there are other signs used in the community. One should be sure to note the sociological characteristics of persons who use different signs. Single sex groups should be worked with first, concentrating on the sex that is the same as that of the investigator. Mixed groups can be extremely profitable later, but only people who show no inhibitions should be selected for these. Sometimes women and men have different signs. Deaf children of signing Deaf parents should be investigated first, and all groups should have one or two Deaf children of Deaf parents as controls.

What I have described requires a lot of effort. But that's what communication is all about: making the effort.

In addition to the matter discussed above, a number of signs in this book have important implications for descriptive and theoretical sociolinguistic and anthropological studies and for applied research in the areas of language and education, language and medicine, and language and law.

IMPLICATIONS FOR SOCIOLINGUISTIC RESEARCH

Signs for sexual behavior have a number of interesting regional and socioethnic variations. A few of these variations are discussed below. All of the variations I have noticed are mentioned in the notes. In New York City, the sign SHOES also means 'male-homosexual'. One sign MALE-MASTURBATION, used in such diverse places as California and Ohio, is often mistaken for SODA-POP in other regions.

Black Southern signs (cf. Woodward 1976) are less generally known to non-Black signers in the U.S., thus when other signers see a Black Southern sign, they often misinterpret it. The Black

Southern sign PREGNANT is identical with a common Northern[1] sign MOTHER, which involves repeated contact with the chin. Southern MOTHER is similar to Black Southern PREGNANT except that MOTHER has a wiggling movement while PREGNANT has repeated contact without wiggling. Black Southern GAY-FEMALE-INTERCOURSE is identical with a White Northern *child* sign HETEROSEXUAL-INTERCOURSE.

One important style variation occurs in the signs for CUNNILINGUS. There are at least three different signs for this activity. One sign is extremely formal, another less formal, and the third very colloquial. It is crucial for the interpreter to find out which sign the client would prefer using. If the wrong sign was chosen for a particular client, lack of communication could result or the client could become insulted.

An example of age variation occurs in the sign ADULTERY; the form with two different handshapes is the older form, and the form with the same (assimilated) handshape is the newer form. Sometimes people of one generation will not immediately catch a form from a different generation. Thus it is important to be aware of historical age variations, when choosing which sign or form of a sign to use.

There are also important interrelationships between regional, ethnic, style, and age variations. For example, the hypothesis suggested by Woodward and Erting (1975), that Southern signers tend to use older forms of signs more often than do Northern signers and that Blacks in the South tend to use historically older forms more often than Whites, was initially guided by the analysis of such items as the Black Southern sign PREGNANT. When this sign was shown to a number of White Southern consultants, only one recognized it. He reported that White signers used to use the sign but now do not. This hypothesis of Woodward and Erting has since been tested and supported (Woodward 1976, Woodward & De Santis 1977).

If Hearing people, especially interpreters, want to establish effective communication with Deaf individuals, they will endeavor to learn what signs are being used by *all* aspects of the Deaf community that they come into contact with. In the notes included with each sign, I have listed all of the regional, ethnic, style, and age variations that I am familiar with for the signs presented. It is crucial that these notes be used when studying these signs.

IMPLICATIONS FOR ANTHROPOLOGICAL RESEARCH

Language use is an extremely important method of maintaining "ethnic" boundaries in the Deaf community - i.e. the distinction Deaf, the ethnically marked group, and Hearing, the majority (Markowicz & Woodward 1978, Padden and Markowicz 1976). Certain characteristics of ASL usage identify a person as Deaf and are reserved for use with other core members of the Deaf community. Because of diglossic pressure, there is very often an immediate shift from such usage to pidgin-like English signing (Woodward 1973, Woodward & Markowicz 1975) when a Hearing person with some knowledge of signing enters a conversation.

Signs for sexual behavior are not well known by the average Hearing signer, apparently not even by many of the most experienced Hearing signers. There is no current general sign manual that provides information about sexual signs, and it was only in 1975 (cf. Woodward 1977) that there was a systematic attempt to incorporate sexual signs into interpreter training programs. One reason for the lack of information in sign manuals and dictionaries (usually prepared by Hearing persons) may be the authoritarianism that Vernon (1972) finds so prevalent in all parts of Deaf education, traditionally controlled by Hearing people. This authoritarianism has often been manifested in self-proclaimed missionary zeal of a number of Hearing people to save Deaf people (cf. Woodward 1975). Another less obvious, but perhaps more compelling, reason for the lack of knowledge of sexual signs on the part of Hearing persons may be that Deaf groups are using sexual signs as a means of preserving the boundaries of the core community. Because these signs represent an area of social intimacy, they may be reserved for use only with core members of the community - those Deaf persons who will probably marry other members.

The pattern of marriage within the Deaf community has been and still is highly endogamous. Fay (1898) reported an 85% rate of endogamous marriages, and Rainer et al. (1963) recorded 95% endogamous marriages of women who were born Deaf, as against 91% of endogamous marriages of women who became Deaf at an early age. It seems then, that a Hearing person, who will almost certainly not marry a Deaf person, is often prevented from successfully penetrating community boundaries into close or intimate relationships with core members. Even Hearing persons who have Deaf parents and have acquired an excellent competence in ASL are often apparently excluded from a knowledge of sexual signs. For the Hearing child of Deaf parents, rites of passage implying full membership in the Deaf community appear to be extremely infrequent. This does not imply of course that the child is not loved; it merely implies that the child is not "REAL-DEAF".

If the hypothesis suggested here is true, and the data presented below on interpreters' evaluations of their own competence in signs for sexual behavior are accurate, then there are important implications for anthropological studies of such factors as rites of passage, social identification and structure, familial and institutional influence on enculturation, and values and beliefs in the Deaf community. Information about these things would be highly useful, because the Deaf community is unique in at least this respect: No more than ten percent of its members are encultured within the nuclear family (Meadow 1972). More recent studies (Karchmer & Trybus 1977) suggest an even lower percentage.

IMPLICATIONS FOR EDUCATION, MEDICINE, AND LAW

As one might expect from the foregoing discussion, signs for sexual behavior are important, and ignorance of them can cause problems in language and education, medicine, and law. In the absence of theoretical information about these signs and practical manuals describing their formation and use, there are no good materials on sex education for Deaf children nor sources where the adult Deaf signer limited in access to English can obtain information about contraception. This lack cannot but affect social, psychiatric, and marriage counseling situations. Several counselors of the Deaf I have talked with have not known of any data on counselors' knowledge of sexual signs, but they felt that this knowledge would be generally low, except perhaps for Hearing counselors who have Deaf parents. I have also received several letters from people involved in sex education and counseling who state that some signs for sexual behavior need to be developed because Deaf people don't have any such signs.

To consider what Deaf signers have, instead of what others say they don't have, I have collected the signs in this book, but this must be regarded as only a subset of the whole class of such signs — e.g. Robert Collins (personal communication) has recently collected some lexically different signs in various parts of Pennsylvania that radically differ from any of the signs discussed in this book.

While data is lacking on sexual signs in education and medicine, there is now some data on signs for sexual behavior and the law. In 1975, I was asked to present what appears to have been the first formal workshop on sexual signs in the U.S. to (Hearing) legal interpreters at the Center for Administrative Justice, Wayne State University, Detroit. I have talked with five of the interpreters since that time. All indicated that they had used the signs they had acquired and one said that these signs were especially useful when he was interpreting in a recent rape case. Again this is somewhat anecdotal evidence, but fortunately in 1976, I was able to gather empirical data from the National Registry of Interpreters for the Deaf (NRID) convention in St. Petersburg, Florida, where I presented some of the signs in this book. One hundred and eight interpreters responded on their knowledge of 71 signs presented here. (Only 8% of these signs were exclusively Southern variants, thus over 90% of the signs are used generally around the country). Woodward (1977) analysed this data and reported that 80.2% of the respondents indicated that all interpreters should definitely know signs for sexual behavior. Eighteen percent said that all interpreters should know these signs, and only two people (1.9%) said that interpreters need not know these signs.

It is very difficult to know how representative the 108 member sample is of the whole number of interpreters: Although the NRID in 1976 did keep some information on its 2,268 members, most was not codified in easily retrievable form. The consultants in this study varied according to sex, race, age, parentage, age of sign acquisition, region, and level of certification. Of the 108, 24 were male and 84 female. The NRID did not know the proportion of female to male interpreters, but believed that the number of females was considerably larger than that of males. There were in this study 105 Whites, 2 Blacks, and 1 Native American. Again, there were no available NRID statistics; however, I have met only six Black interpreters (two at this NRID meeting) in eight years of research and teaching. Forty-five Black Deaf consultants I have worked with in Georgia could not name one Black Hearing signer that they could use for interpreting purposes.

Of the respondents, 62% were certified, as compared to 39.7% of the total NRID membership, in April 1976. Provisional certification was 4.6% compared with 0.9% in the NRID. In the group of respondents, 17.6% had various intermediate levels of certification, as compared with 22% of the total NRID membership. Finally, 39.8% of the respondents held the *then* highest certification (CSC), as compared with 17.2% of the total NRID group. The sample here is thus more heavily weighted for highly certified people and less heavily weighted for those uncertified than was the total NRID membership of that time. Thus we might expect better knowledge in this sample than from a more representative sampling of the NRID.

However, mean scores for reported knowledge were very low. For the 71 signs demonstrated, over one fifth of the interpreters reported no competence in signs for sexual excitement (which could be particularly detrimental in rape cases), one fourth reported no competence in signs for other sexual activity, and over one half claimed they knew no signs for homosexual behavior. 73% of the interpreters knew less than half the presented signs for sexual excitement and heterosexual behavior, 85% knew less than half the signs for other sexual activity, while 92% knew less than half the signs for homosexual activity. Again the most striking aspect of this low level of knowledge in this semantic area of signing is that this sample of interpreters contained a higher proportion of highly certified interpreters and a lower proportion of uncertified interpreters than was shown in the total National Registry of Interpreters for the Deaf membership for that time. As expected, however, if the interpreter was more highly certified, had Deaf parents, and acquired signs at an early age, the scores were significantly higher than if the interpreter had none of these characteristics.

There are a few other interesting generalizations that can be made from the data on individual signs. Wherever a Black Southern sign variant appeared in the list, it was always reported as known less well than any other variant. After Black Southern variants, White Southern variants were known less well by the NRID interpreters studied than any other regional variants. This trend continued with other specifically regional variants, which in turn were known less well than so called standard (i.e. 'more like educated Gallaudet signers') signs. This situation is particularly unfortunate, because Deaf people who know the 'standard' educated signs have less need for interpreters to know signs for sexual behavior; these deaf persons generally understand and might prefer the English word fingerspelled to the sign. Uneducated Deaf persons, especially those who are Black Southerners, will be less likely to understand the fingerspelled English word or 'standard' sign that some interpreters know; they are also more likely, because of their poor competence in White Hearing English, to be mistreated in legal situtations whether it be arrest or trial proceedings.

It would seem that knowledge of sexual signs is highly desired, but not too often attained. Hopefully, books such as this one, especially discussed by skilled Deaf signers, will help alleviate this lack of knowledge in individuals who need competence in these signs.

SIGN ILLUSTRATIONS

Notes on the signs collected for sexual behavior appear with each drawing. These notes should be used in conjuction with the sign drawings. Several cautions about these signs must be made here again. THESE ARE ONLY *SOME* SIGNS FOR SEXUAL BEHAVIOR. THEY DO NOT INCLUDE ALL SIGNS FOR SEXUAL BEHAVIOR OR ALL VARIANTS. THEY MAY OR MAY NOT BE USED IN A GIVEN COMMUNITY. IT IS THE RESPONSIBILITY OF THE PERSON USING THIS BOOK TO FIND OUT WHAT IS BEING USED IN A GIVEN COMMUNITY.

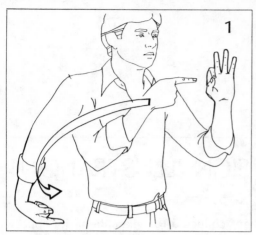

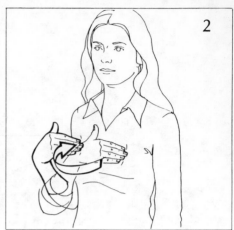

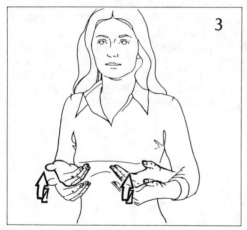

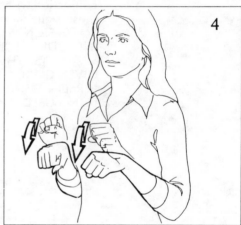

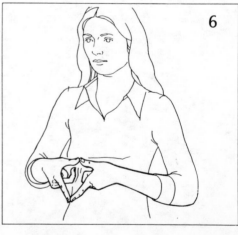

BODY PARTS

1 ANUS

A number of Deaf people do not have a sign for this body part; they ususally fingerspell A-N-U-S or A-S-S-H-O-L-E. The pointing to the buttocks is not obligatory.

2 BREASTS (1)

This is a common sign for breasts.

3 BREASTS (2)

This is another common sign for breasts. For the singular form, BREAST, use only one hand.

4 BREASTS (3) (bouncing)

This sign generally refers to movement of the breasts and is more restricted in use than the other signs for breasts.

5 CLITORIS (1)

This variant seems to be the most widely used. It is very similar to the sign for vagina, but also requires the extension and wiggling of the thumb of the dominant hand.[2]

6 CLITORIS (2)

This variant is used in California and may be used in other places.

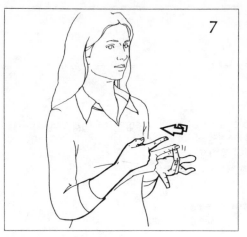

7

8

9

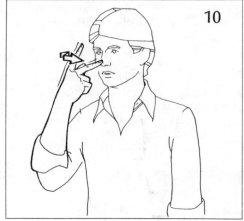

10

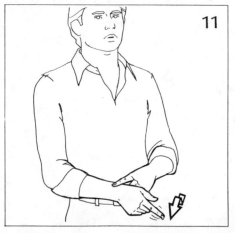

11

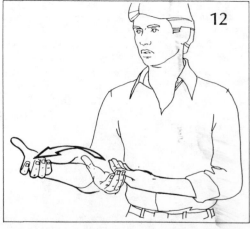

12

7 CLITORIS (3)

This is a third variation for clitoris. It looks similar to the sign CUT-CLASSES. However, CLITORIS (3) has the palm of the non-dominant hand facing upward. This sign is used in Arizona and perhaps other places.

8 NIPPLES

This sign is the same as BREASTS (1), except that NIPPLES has an "F" handshape. There is another sign for nipple-erection.

9 PEE

This is an intialized and therefore more English-like sign. In some regions of the country it means both PEE and PENIS. Some signers do make a distinction between them through facial expression and movement repetition. PEE has the facial expression and quick single movement shown in drawing 9, while PENIS has a neutral facial expression and a double movement as shown in drawing 10.[3]

10 PENIS (1)

This is the common initialized sign PENIS. Please read the note for PEE (sign 9).

11 PENIS (2)

This is the common uninitialized sign for penis. The non-dominant hand may be on top of or underneath the dominant hand. This sign also involves a wiggling motion of the dominant hand or no movement at all. If there is only one upward motion, the sign means ERECTION-OF-PENIS.

12 PENIS (3)

This sign for penis is used but would be unappropriate for most courtroom situations. It really means WELL-HUNG-PENIS Without facial expression, it is also a commonly used sign for animal penises.

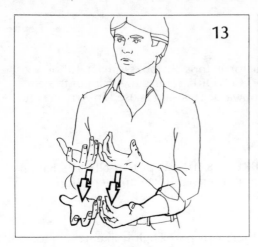

13

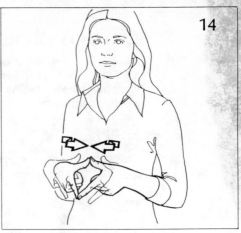

14

15

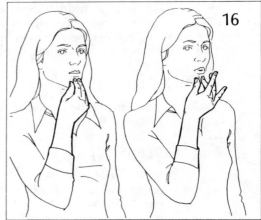

16

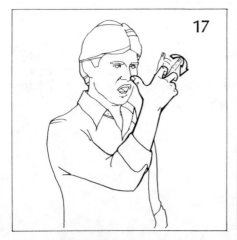

17

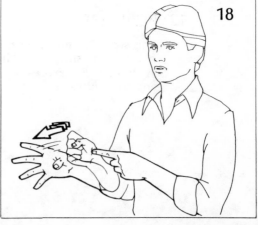

18

13 TESTES, TESTICLES

This sign is used for testes, testicles, or balls. The motion may also be alternating.

14 VAGINA (1)

This is the most commonly used sign for vagina. Most Deaf people suggest pointing the index fingers downward to avoid any possible confusion with the sign TRIANGLE, which normally has the index fingers pointing upward.

15 VAGINA (2)

This sign is somewhat less common than the previous sign. It is sometimes used in Southern areas and other areas as well.

16 VAGINA (3)

This is a third variant for vagina. It is used less frequently than the other two variants. The only people that have been found using this sign are Black Deaf people in Georgia.

SEXUAL EXCITEMENT

17 CLIMAX

This sign is done on the nose and can mean male or female climax. It can also be signed with two hands. This sign can be combined with sign 31 to form the compound SEXUAL EXCITEMENT + CLIMAX.[4]

18 EJACULATION (1)

This sign has several variants. The non-dominant hand can point to the dominant hand with a "G" or "I" handshape. Some people say the difference is in the different sizes of the penis, other people vary where they touch, depending on the intensity of the climax. All variants should be done with repeated movement. A single movement often means SEMEN.

22

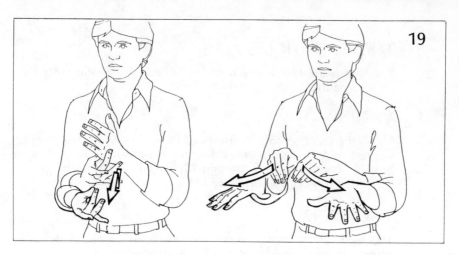

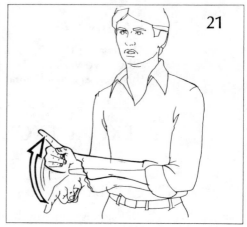

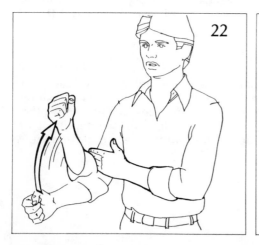

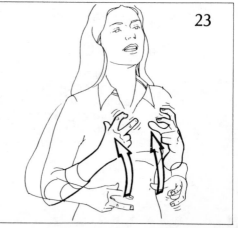

19 EJACULATION (2)

This is a very interesting compound of the signs for GRAVY and SPREAD, still used by some Black signers in Georgia.

20 EJACULATION-INSIDE-VAGINA

Note that the non-dominant hand grasps the dominant wrist. This sign only means 'ejaculation-inside-the-vagina'.

21 ERECTION-OF-PENIS (1)

This is one variant for erection of penis. It is based on sign number 11, PENIS. For erection, there is one upward movement.

22 ERECTION-OF-PENIS (2)

This sign is not considered as polite as the previous sign.

23 FEMALE-CLIMAX

This sign is used in California and perhaps elsewhere. It is done with a "3" handshape and moves up both sides of the front of the body. Some signers may use a downward instead of an upward movement. This sign means female climax only.

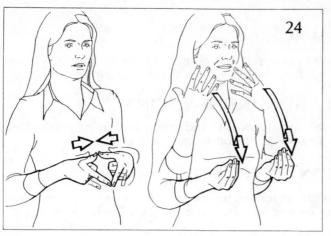

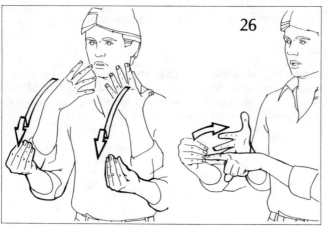

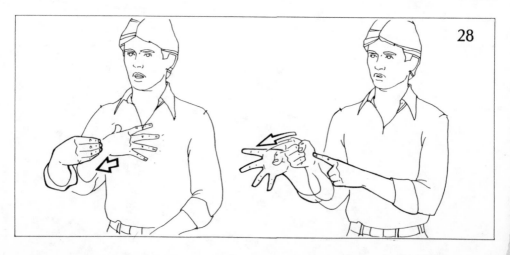

24 FEMALE-LUBRICATION

This is a compound of the signs for VAGINA and WET.

25 HORNY

This is one sign used for this meaning. See also signs 29 and 30.

26 MALE-LUBRICATION

This is a compound of the signs WET and WETNESS-SPREADING-OVER-PENIS.

27 NIPPLE-ERECTION

The movement of this sign may be repeated but one movement is sufficient.

28 SEMEN

This is a compound of the sign WHITE, not obligatory, and a sign similar to EJACULATION. The second part of this compound has only one movement. Remember the sign EJACULATION requires repeated movements.

29

30

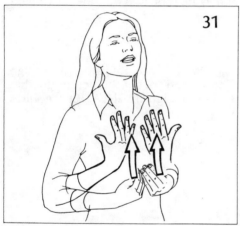

31

32

33

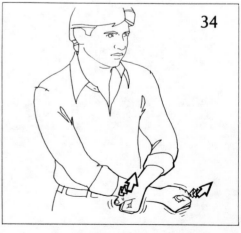

34

29 SEXUAL-DESIRE (1)

This variant is similar to the sign HUNGRY. However, the facial expression is different and repetition is added. The sign HUNGRY has only one downward movement.

30 SEXUAL-DESIRE (2)

This variant is similar to the sign THIRSTY, but differs in facial expression.

31 SEXUAL-EXCITEMENT

This sign may be used in a number of different compounds.

MASTURBATION

32 CLITORAL-MASTURBATION

This is a one-handed non-directional sign.[5]

33 GAY-FEMALE-MUTUAL-VAGINAL-MASTURBATION

Both hands cross and perform the sign for VAGINAL-MASTURBATION (sign 38) with "open 8" handshapes.

34 GAY-MALE-MUTUAL-MASTURBATION

Both hands cross and perform the sign for MALE-MASTURBATION (sign 35) with "S" handshapes.

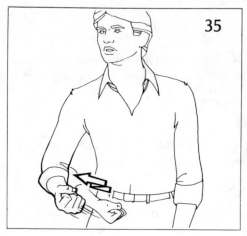

35

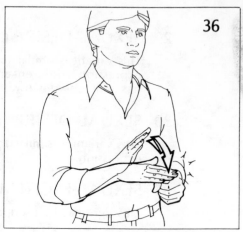

36

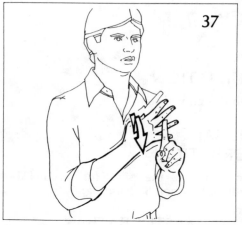

37

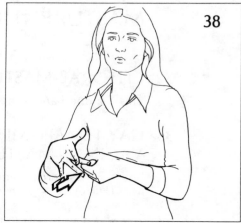

38

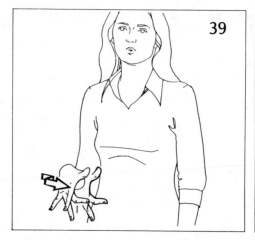

39

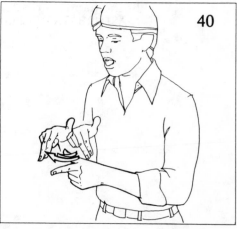

40

35 MALE-MASTURBATION (1)

This is the most common sign used. It is made with one active hand with or without a passive non-dominant hand.[6] This is a directional sign.

36 MALE-MASTURBATION (2)

This is a regional variant, found in such diverse places as California and Ohio. It looks very similar to some signs for soda pop, so be careful of the distinction.

37 MALE-MASTURBATION (3)

This is a variant that seems to be limited to White Georgia signers.

38 VAGINAL-MASTURBATION (1)

This sign is directional with the sign pointed towards the actor-receiver.

39 VAGINAL-MASTURBATION (2)

This is also a directional sign.

ORAL SEX

40 CUNNILINGUS (1)

This is the most polite and formal of three variants. It is an incorporated compound of LICK + VAGINA. The sign can be made without tongue extension.

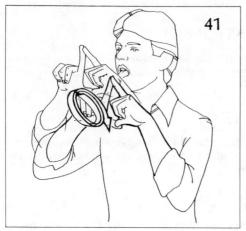

41

42

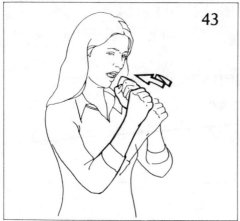

43

44

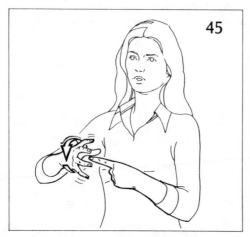

45

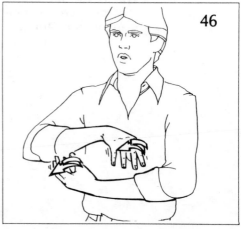

46

41 CUNNILINGUS (2)

This is a somewhat less formal sign than the previous sign. It is most often done with tongue movement.

42 CUNNILINGUS (3)

This is the least formal of the three variants. This sign requires tongue movement. It would not be appropriate for most courtroom situations, unless the client did not understand other variants.

43 FELLATIO (1)

This is a commonly used variant that can be done with one or two hands.

44 FELLATIO (2)

This variant can also be done with one or two hands but the tongue movement in the mouth is required.

45 FELLATIO (3)

This is a sign used primarily in California. Some people prefer to sign it as a compound with a point to the mouth first for added clarity.

46 GAY-MALE-MUTUAL-ORAL-SEX

This sign can only be used for males performing oral sex on each other.

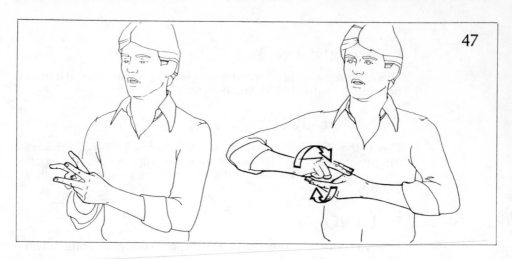

47

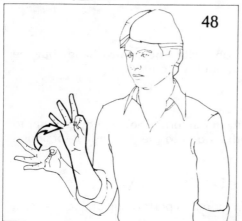

48

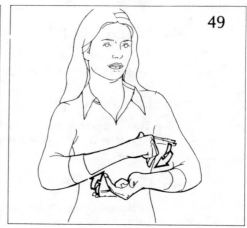

49

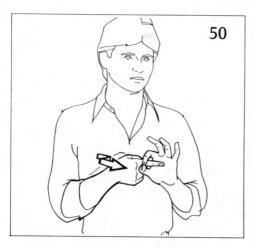

50

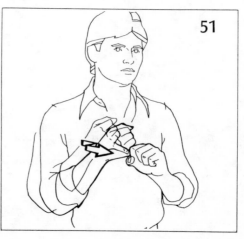

51

47 MUTUAL-ORAL-SEX, SIXTY-NINE (1)

This is a commonly used sign that is related to the sign INTERCOURSE, FUCK (sign 58).

48 MUTUAL-ORAL-SEX, SIXTY-NINE (2)

Young well-educated signers will often fingerspell "6-9". Notice here that a twisting motion has been added that makes it a more sign-like unit (cf. Battison 1978).

49 MUTUAL-ORAL-SEX, SIXTY-NINE (3)

This is a fairly common sign in isolation. It is frequently preferred in sign compounds like LESBIAN + MUTUAL-ORAL-SEX.

INTERCOURSE

50 ANAL-INTERCOURSE (1)

This sign is used for activity between a male and a female. Never use a "G" into an "O" handshape for ANAL-INTERCOURSE, since that means vaginal-intercourse.

51 ANAL-INTERCOURSE (2)

The note for sign 50 applies to this variant also.

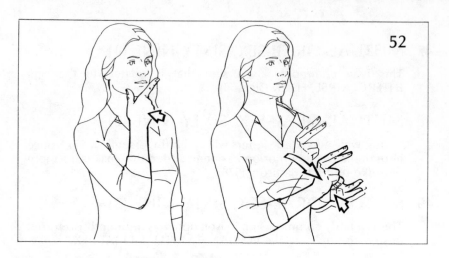

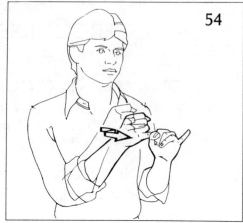

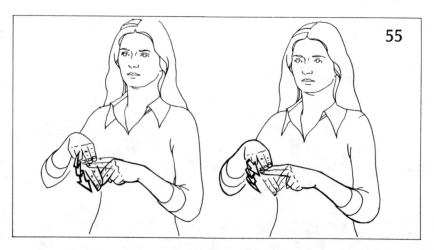

52 GAY-FEMALE-INTERCOURSE (1)

The most common sign for this activity is a compound of the signs LESBIAN and FUCK. The sign for BALL may be used instead of FUCK.

53 GAY-FEMALE-INTERCOURSE (2)

This is a Black Georgian sign. It is identical to the White Northern child-sign for sexual activity between any two people.

54 GAY-MALE-INTERCOURSE

This sign is very common.

55 INTERCOURSE

This is a polite Black Southern variant. The right hand fingers make a short downward movement to touch the left hand fingers, which then bend slightly. This progression repeats until the left hand fingers are very bent. This series of movements is then reversed until the left hand fingers are again straight.

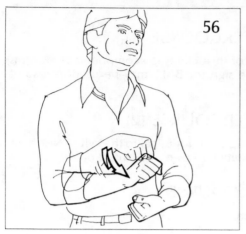

56

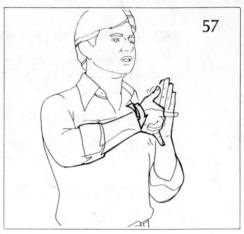

57

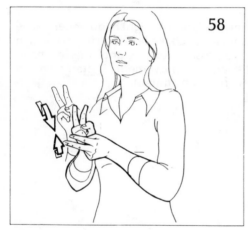

58

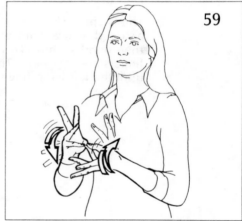

59

60

61

56 INTERCOURSE, BALL (1)

This is also a very common sign, perhaps used more among younger Deaf people.

57 INTERCOURSE, BALL (2)

This is a Black Georgian variant similar in meaning to sign 56.

58 INTERCOURSE, FUCK (1)

A commonly used sign, that is sometimes translated 'fuck' although the sign is not that strong in comparison to the English word.

59 INTERCOURSE, FUCK (2)

This is a Black Georgian variant that is related to sign 58.

60 INTERCOURSE, LAY (1)

The exact usage of this sign is unclear, but it seems to carry the connotation of the English word "lay" or "have someone sexually."

61 INTERCOURSE, LAY (2)

The note for sign 60 applies to this variant also.

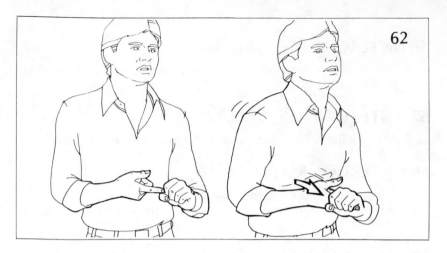

62

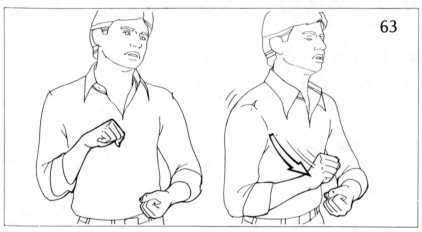

63

64

62 PENETRATION (1)

With a sharp movement (as shown), this sign would be appropriate in a rape case. With a less sharp movement, and perhaps with the sign SUCCESS added, it would be appropriate for discussing sexual activities between consenting partners.

63 PENETRATION (2)

With a sharp movement (as shown), this sign would also be appropriate in a rape case. A "sharp" movement like this is performed with speed and a lunge forward with the shoulder.

OTHER SEXUAL ACTIVITY

64 BE-RAPED

This is a North Carolina variant. It is done on the side of the neck. The sign STUCK with the extended connotation of CARELESS-PREGNANCY (see sign 102), is done in the middle of the neck.

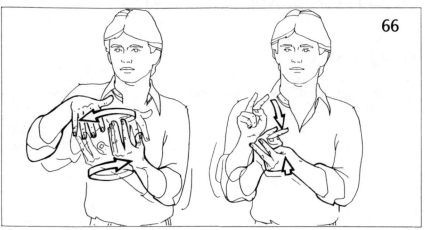

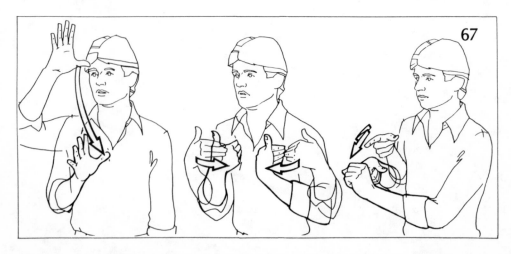

65 FEMALE-BESTIALITY

Name the woman, the type of animal, and then the sign FUCK. In some areas the sign for BALL may be used instead of the sign FUCK.

66 GROUP-SEX

This meaning is signed INTERMINGLE plus the sign or signs for the type of activity. The most generally used sign is FUCK or BALL.

67 MALE-BESTIALITY

Name the man, the type of animal, and then sign PENETRATION with repetition.

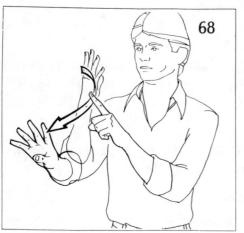

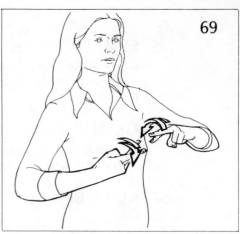

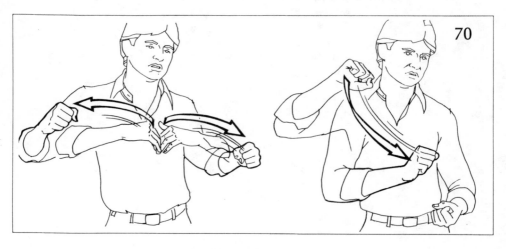

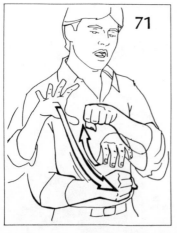

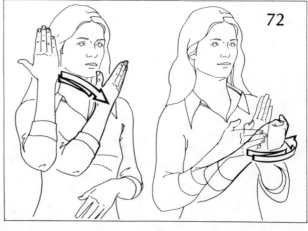

68 MANY-MEN-USING-ONE-WOMAN

This was the only sign found during this research.

69 MATE-SWAPPING

This variant generally means swapping between two couples. Numbers can be incorporated to add to the number of couples involved.

70 RAPE (1)

This is probably one of the most widely understood and used signs for rape. It is crucial to include the first part of the compound shown here or the sign FORCE. There are probably regional variations, so check in your community.

71 RAPE (2)

This is another commonly used sign for rape.

INDIVIDUALS AND RELATIONSHIPS

72 ADULTERY

Sometimes this is a compound sign of HIDDEN-FROM-SIGHT (not obligatory) and ADULTERY. Older signers use the older form of the sign ADULTERY which had a "G" handshape for the dominant hand. Younger signers tend to use the newer assimilated form using two "B" handshapes.

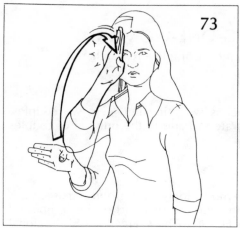

73

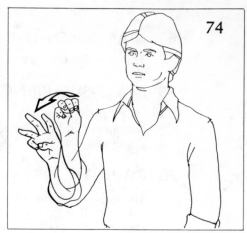

74

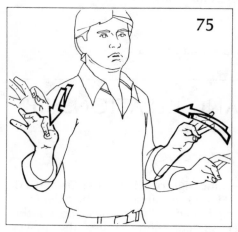

75

76

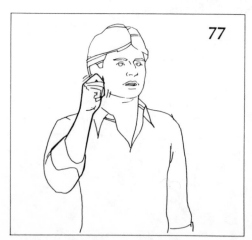

77

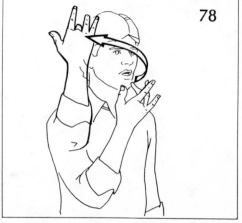

78

73 BUTCH

This is an extended meaning of the sign BASTARD.

74 COMMON-LAW-RELATIONSHIP

Here is another example of fingerspelling, "M-W", that with the addition of movement becomes a more sign-like unit (see Battison 1978).

75 EFFEMINATE

This is a somewhat derogatory sign. In some areas it means MODEL, in others it means SISSY, and in others EFFEMINATE-GAY-MALE.

76 FORNICATION

This is a compound of the sign HIDDEN-FROM-SIGHT and the sign INTERCOURSE, BALL (sign 56).

77 GAY (1)

This sign is traditionally used only between Gay (homosexual) people. A few Straight people in the East, however, use the sign to refer to Gay people. A number of highly educated Gay people prefer the fingerspelled version, "G-A-Y".

78 GAY-MALE (1)

This is the most common sign, even though to some people it is derogatory. With a neutral facial expression, it is less offensive.

79

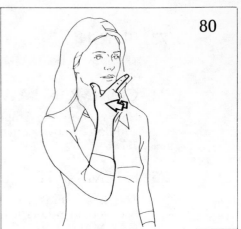

80

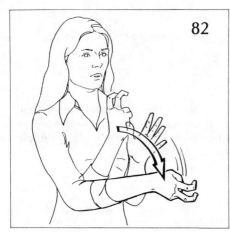

82

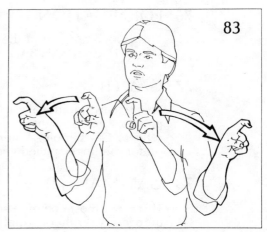

83

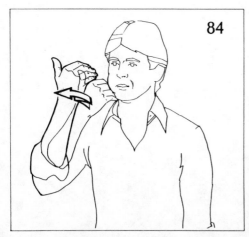

84

85

79 GAY-MALE (2)

This is a rarely found sign.

80 GAY-FEMALE, LESBIAN

This is a common sign with the hand in this orientation.

81 INCEST

There is no illustration shown here because one must simply name the family members involved and then the activity. (e.g. FATHER + DAUGHTER + INTERCOURSE).

82 PROMISCUOUS-PERSON

This sign can be used for both males and females.

83 PROMISCUOUS-WOMAN

This sign is used to refer to women only. It can also mean an "easy lay".

84 PROSTITUTE

This is the only sign found, but it seems to be fairly widespread.

85 QUEER, GAY (2)

With a neutral facial expression, as shown, this sign is not derogatory in California, but still tends to be derogatory in the East. With a derogatory facial expression the sign becomes very derogatory in all places and should be avoided unless one wished to be insulting.

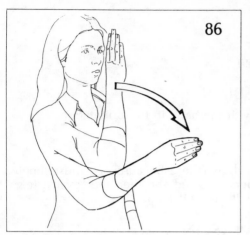

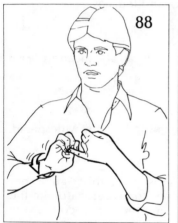

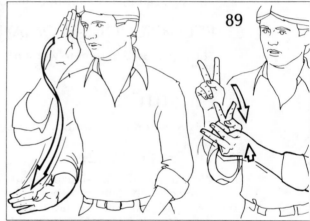

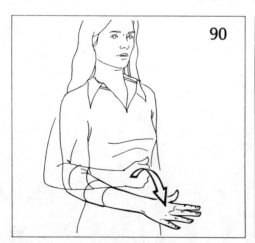

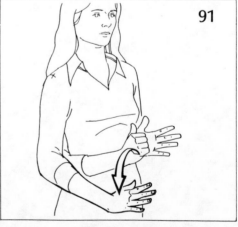

86 STRAIGHT (heterosexual)

This was the only variant found during this research.

87 VIRGIN (1)

This is an initialized sign. It is probably better to use with people who prefer English.

88 VIRGIN (2)

This is the sign CHERRY, and like the English word 'cherry' can have the extended meaning 'virgin'.

89 VIRGIN (3)

This is signed NEVER + INTERCOURSE and can also be signed HASN'T + INTERCOURSE. VIRGIN 2 and 3 are uninitialized signs and are more preferable for non-English Deaf people. Check in your community for other possible signs.

BIRTH CONTROL

90 ABORTION (1)

This is a common sign for abortion. For added clarity it can be signed as the compound BABY + ABORTION.

91 ABORTION (2)

This is another common sign for abortion that can also be used in a compound form as explained for abortion 1.

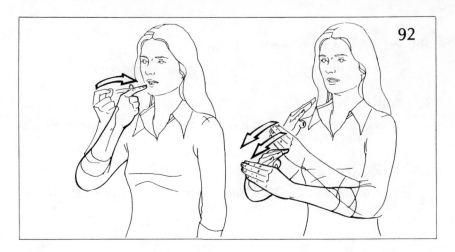

92

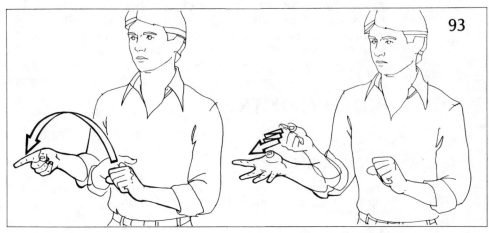

93

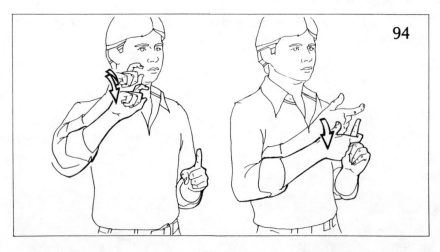

94

92 BIRTH-CONTROL-PILL

This is signed as the compound PILL + PREVENT. It can also be signed "B-C" + PILL or merely "B-C".

93 COITUS-INTERRUPTUS

This is the compound sign WITHDRAWAL-OF-PENIS + EJACULATION.

94 CONDOM (1)

This is the compound sign RUBBER + HOOK-OVER-PENIS. This seems to be the most common variant.

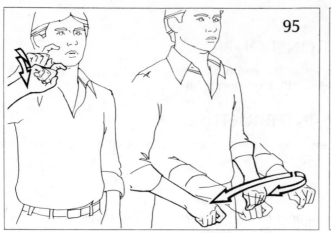

95

96

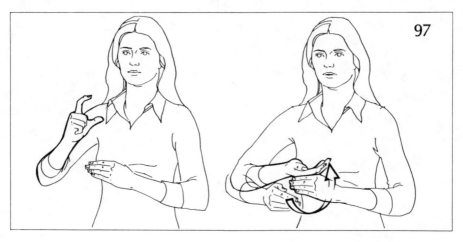

97

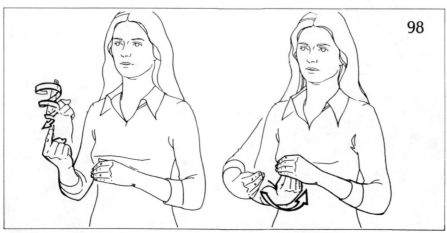

98

95 CONDOM (2)

This is another compound sign, RUBBER+STRETCH-OVER-PENIS. The sign RUBBER alone, like the English word 'rubber', can have the extended meaning 'condom'.

96 CONTRACEPTIVE-FOAM

This is one possible variant, but many people seem to have several variations. Making a compound with some variation of the signs INJECT-FOAM and "B-C" or PREVENT is common.

97 DIAPHRAGM

This is the compound sign ROUND-SHAPED + INSERT-IN-VAGINA. (B)

98 IUD (Intra-Uterine-Device)

This is the compound sign SPIRAL-SHAPED + INSERT-IN-VAGINA. This can also be fingerspelled I-U-D.

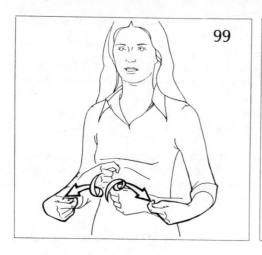

99

100

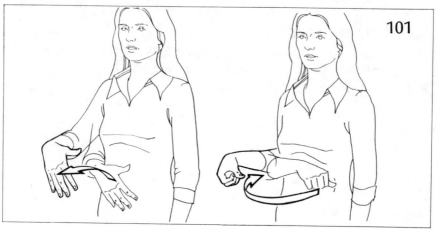

101

102

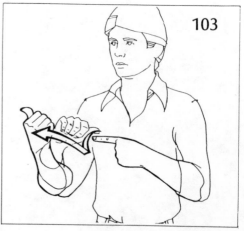

103

99 STERILIZATION, TUBAL-LIGATION, VASECTOMY

This sign can be signed alone or as the compound MAN + TIE or WOMAN + TIE. Make sure that TIE is signed at the waist.

100 WITHDRAWAL (of-penis)

If this sign is used, there was definitely no ejaculation inside the vagina. However, this sign does not specify whether or not ejaculation takes place outside the vagina.

HEALTH, HYGIENE, AND FUNCTION

101 CAESAREAN

This is the compound sign PREGNANT + STOMACH-OPERATION. Another possible compound sign is STOMACH-OPERATION + BIRTH.

102 CARELESS-PREGNANCY

This sign means 'careless' or 'unexpected' pregnancy.

103 CIRCUMCISION

There are two variants of this sign. As shown here, the older variant uses a "G" handshape on the non-dominant hand and an "A" handshape on the dominant hand. The newer variant uses assimilated handshapes, two "A" hands.

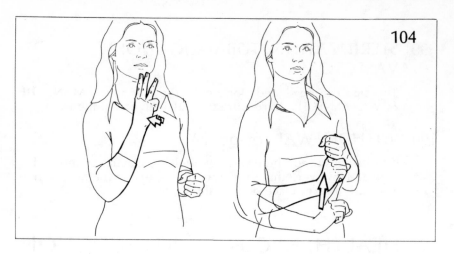

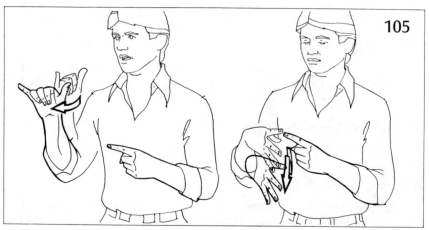

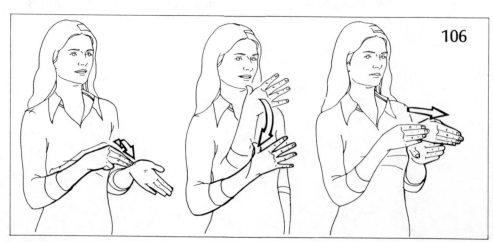

104 DOUCHE

This is the compound sign WATER + STICK-IN-VAGINA. Note the difference between this sign and ENEMA (sign 126).

105 GONORRHEA

This is the compound sign YELLOW + DISCHARGE-FROM-PENIS. This sign is only appropriate for use for male gonorrhea. For females, fingerspelling "V-D" would be appropriate.

106 GYNECOLOGIST

This is the compound sign DOCTOR + WOMAN + SPECIALIZE. The sign DOCTOR is probably best understood for most signers as the non-initialized form that is shown here.

58

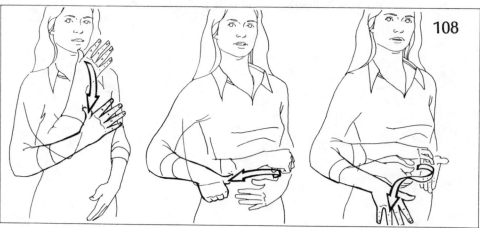

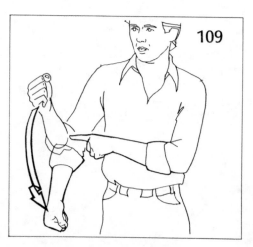

107 HOT-FLASHES

This is a compound sign. The second part of the compound looks like the sign for SEXUAL-EXCITEMENT, however, the facial expression is different.

108 HYSTERECTOMY

This is the compound sign WOMAN + STOMACH-OPERATE + REMOVE-FROM-STOMACH.

109 IMPOTENT (male)

This sign is related to the non-formal sign for ERECTION-OF-PENIS (sign 22).

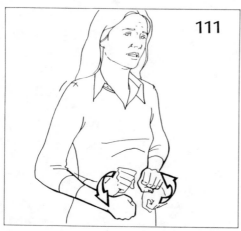

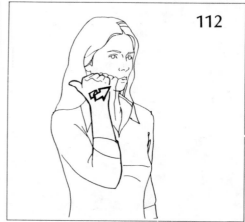

110 MENOPAUSE

This is the compound sign OLD + MENSTRUATION + STOP.

111 MENSTRUAL-CRAMPS

Be sure that this is signed at the waist.

112 MENSTRUATION

This is a common sign for menstruation. In intimate or 'whisper' situations, there is a variant done by only puffing the cheek repeatedly.

113 MISCARRIAGE

This sign can be done alone or as the compound sign BABY + MISCARRIAGE.

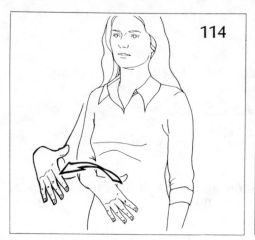

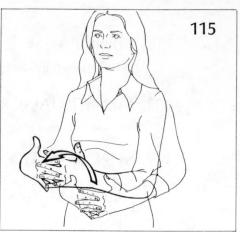

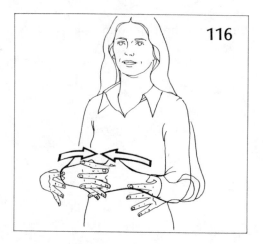

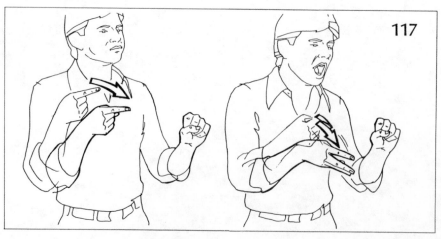

114 PREGNANT (1)

This is a common sign for pregnant.

115 PREGNANT (2)

This is also a common sign for pregnant.

116 PREGNANT (3)

This is a common sign for pregnant, although in some areas of the country it can mean 'intercourse'. If this is true in your area, then check to see what sign is preferred for pregnant.

SPECIAL NOTE: Some Black signers from Georgia use a sign for PREGNANT, identical with the common Northern sign MOTHER, which repeatedly contacts the "5" handshape on the chin. The Southern sign MOTHER similarly uses the "5" handshape, but holds the contact on the chin while the loose fingers wiggle. Black Georgian PREGNANT is an older sign and was previously used by some Whites in the South. At the time of this research this sign was only being used among some Black Georgian signers.

117 PREMATURE-EJACULATION

This was the only variant found during this research.

118

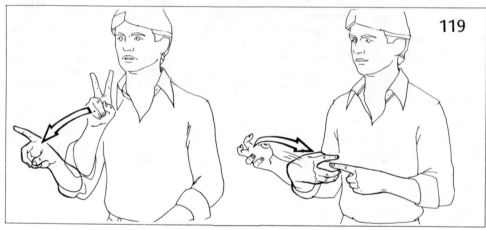

119

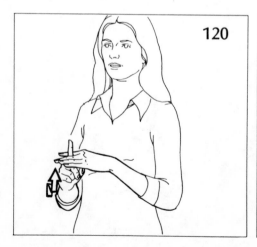

120

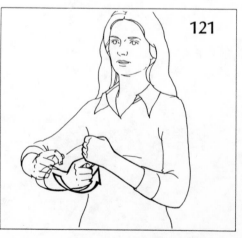

121

118 SANITARY-NAPKIN

This compound seems to be very common.

119 SYPHILIS

This is a compound of "V-D" and a sign involving PENIS. This sign can only be used for male syphilis. For females, fingerspelling "V-D" only would be appropriate.

120 TAMPON (1)

This is one of the variants found.

121 TAMPON (2)

This is another variant. These two signs for TAMPON do not seem to be as widely accepted as the sign for SANITARY-NAPKIN.

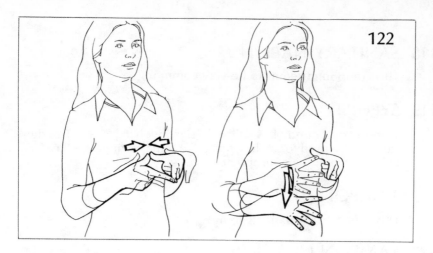

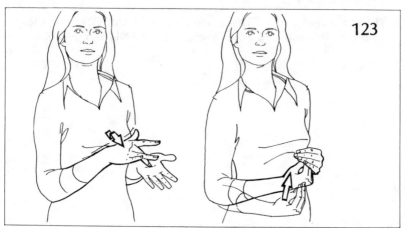

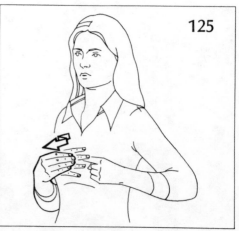

122 VAGINAL-DISCHARGE

This is the compound sign VAGINA + DISCHARGE-FROM-VAGINA. This sign for 'fluid-running' is very common in ASL and can be found in incorporated compounds like BLOOD, NOSE-RUNNING, WATER-RUNNING and earlier in this book for the sign GONORRHEA.

123 VAGINAL-SUPPOSITORY

This is the compound sign MEDICINE + INSERT-IN-VAGINA.

OTHER SIGNS

124 BREAST-SUCKING (1) (sexual)

This sign may be done with or without a passive "B" hand on the chest. If a "B" hand is used, it must be between the chest and the active hand. If the passive "B" hand is on the outside of the active hand, the sign means BREAST-FEEDING.

125 BREAST-SUCKING (2) (sexual)

This is another common sign for this meaning.

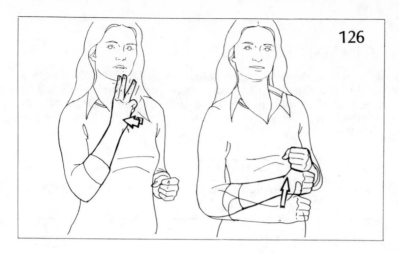

126

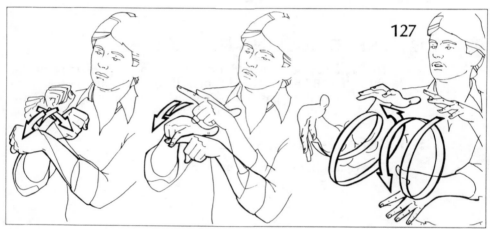

127

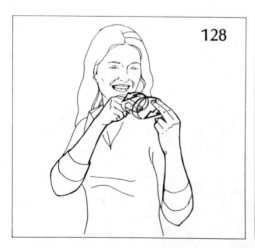

128

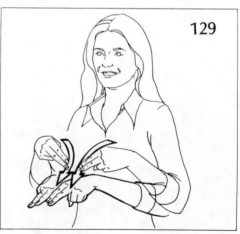

129

126 ENEMA

This is the compound sign WATER + STICK-UP-ANUS. Note the difference between this sign and DOUCHE (sign 104).

127 FOREPLAY

This is the compound sign NECKING + DRY-FUCKING + BODY-CARESSING.

128 FRENCH-KISSING

This is a very common sign.

129 GO-TO-BED-TOGETHER

This is a euphemistic sign meaning 'to have sexual relations with someone' or 'to go to bed with someone'.

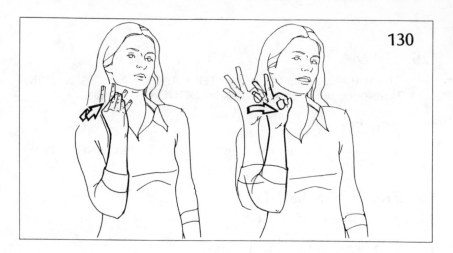

130

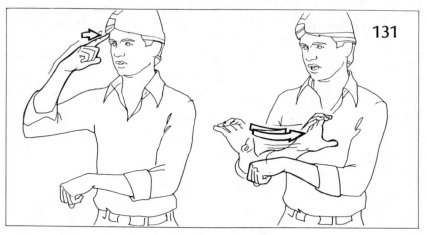

131

130 HICKEY

This is the compound sign SUCK-NECK + MARK-ON-NECK.

131 THINK-DIRTY-THOUGHTS

No other variants of this sign were found during this research.

FOOTNOTES

1 The term "Northern" in this book does not refer to one specific region of the country but rather to all regions other than the Southeastern part of the United States.

2 For a right handed signer the "dominant" hand is the right hand and the "non-dominant" hand is the left hand. For the left handed signer it is the exact opposite.

3 Supalla and Newport (1978) have discussed a number of similar noun-verb pairs, where the verb has one movement and the noun has repeated movements. A good example would be the noun-verb pair CHAIR and SIT.

4 Compound signs are not usually just the juxtaposition of two or more basic signs. Movement and handshape may be very different in a compound. It is important to pay close attention to the illustrations to notice any difference between a sign used in its basic form and the same sign used in a compound.

5 "Directionality" is an ASL verb inflection. Directional signs move from the agent/actor (or a point in his/her direction) toward the receiver (or a point in his/her direction). A good example would be the signs I-GIVE-YOU and YOU-GIVE-ME. These are each a single sign unit, one moving from me toward you, and the other moving from you toward me. Non-directional signs cannot utilize the directional inflection.

6 In a particular sign, the "active hand" will be the one that moves and the "passive hand" will not move.

BIBLIOGRAPHY

Battison, R. 1978. *Lexical Borrowing in American Sign Language*, Silver Spring, Md.: Linstok Press.

Fay, A. 1898. *Marriages of the Deaf in America*, Washington, D.C.: Volta Bureau.

Karchmer, M. and R. Trybus. 1972. Who Are the Deaf Children in Mainstream Programs ?, Washington, D.C.: Gallaudet College, Office of Demographic Studies.

Markowicz, H. and J. Woodward. 1978. Language and the Maintenance of Ethnic Boundaries in the Deaf Community, *Communication and Cognition*, (Special Issue on Sign Language, Ronnie Wilbur, ed.)

Meadow, K. 1972. Sociolinguistics, Sign Language, and the Deaf Subculture, in T. O'Rourke, ed., *Psycholinguistics and Total Communication: The State of the Art*, Washington, D.C.: American Annals of the Deaf, 19-33.

Padden, C. and H. Markowicz. 1976. Cultural Conflicts Between Hearing and Deaf Communities, in F. and A. Crammattee, eds., *VII World Congress of the World Federation of the Deaf*, Silver Spring, Md.: National Association of the Deaf, 407-411.

Rainer, J., K. Altschuler, and F. Kallman. 1963. *Family and Mental Health in a Deaf Population*, New York: State Psychiatric Institute, Columbia University.

Supalla, T. and E. Newport. 1978. How Many Seats in a Chair? The Derivation of Nouns and Verbs in American Sign Language, in P. Siple, ed., *Understanding Language Through Sign Language Research*, New York: Academic Press, 91-132.

Vernon, M. 1972. Non-linguistic Aspects of Sign Language, Human Feelings, and Thought Processes, in T. O'Rourke, ed., *Psycholinguistics and Total Communication: The State of the Art,* Washington, D.C.: American Annals of the Deaf, 11-18.

Woodward, J. 1973. Some Characteristics of Pidgin Sign English, *Sign Language Studies* 3, 39-46.

Woodward, J. 1975. How You Gonna Get to Heaven if You Can't Talk with Jesus: the Educational Establishment vs. The Deaf Community. A paper presented at the annual meeting of the Society for Applied Anthropology, Amsterdam, March.

Woodward, J. 1976. Black Southern Signing, *Language in Society* 5, 211-218.

Woodward, J. 1977. Sex is Definitely a Problem: Interpreters' Knowledge of Signs for Sexual Behavior, *Sign Language Studies* 14, 73-88.

Woodward, J. and S. De Santis. 1977. Two to One it Happens: Dynamic Phonology in Two Sign Languages, *Sign Language Studies* 17, 329-346.

Woodward, J. and C. Erting. 1975. Synchronic Variation and Historical Change in American Sign Language, *Language Sciences* 37, 9-12.

Woodward, J. and H. Markowicz. 1975. Some Handy New Ideas on Pidgin and Creoles: Pidgin Sign Languages. A paper presented at the 1975 International Conference on Pidgin and Creole Languages, Honolulu, January.

SIGN INDEX

The number given with each sign listing is the sign number, not the page number.

PERSONAL NOTES

We encourage you to use this space for recording of signs and/or variations preferred by your local Deaf community.

_____

_____

_____

_____

_____

_____

_____

_____

_____

_____

_____

_____

_____

_____

_____

_____

_____

_____

_____

_____

_____

_____

_____

PERSONAL NOTES

We encourage you to use this space for recording of signs and/or variations preferred by your local Deaf community.

_____

_____

_____

_____

_____

_____

_____

_____

_____

_____

_____

_____

_____

_____

_____

_____

_____

_____

_____

_____

_____

_____

PERSONAL NOTES

We encourage you to use this space for recording of signs and/or variations preferred by your local Deaf community.